Test Book *for*

Wordly Wise 3000

Book 5

Educators Publishing Service

Cambridge and Toronto

Guidelines for EPS Reproducible Books

Educators Publishing Service is pleased to offer this publication as a "reproducible book."

EPS grants the individual instructor who has purchased this book the right to make sufficient copies of reproducible pages for use by all students in his or her classroom. This permission is limited to the purchaser or owner of the book and does not apply to entire grades, schools, or school systems. No part of this publication may be transmitted, stored, or recorded in any form without written permission from the publisher. Copying of the book or its parts for resale is prohibited.

To order additional copies of this book, please call our Customer Service department at 1.800.225.5750. You can also place an order online at www.epsbooks.com.

Written by Robyn Raymer
Design and typesetting by Rebecca C. Royen

Editor: Stacey L. Nichols
Managing Editor: Sheila Neylon

Book 5, Lesson 1 Test

Choose the BEST way to complete each sentence or answer each question. Circle the letter of your answer.

1. Which is an example of someone with <u>resilience</u>?

    a someone who gets good grades in school

    b someone who is a very talented artist and writer

    c someone who gets well quickly after an illness

    d someone who is able to memorize facts easily

2. In the spring, our town has a <u>pervasive</u> scent of flowers blooming. This means that the scent

    a is lovely.

    b is unpleasant.

    c can be smelled throughout town.

    d is too sweet.

3. Drivers experienced a <u>rebuff</u> as they traveled down the highway. The highway was

    a many lanes wide.

    b closed due to a landslide.

    c the quickest route to the nearest city.

    d recently paved.

4. Our puppy is <u>avid</u> for our attention. This means that she

    a is greedy for attention.

    b stands at attention.

    c doesn't obey commands.

    d is very obedient.

5. From his <u>brusqueness</u> on the phone, I could tell that Dan was upset. Dan spoke

    a absentmindedly.

    b in a silly way.

    c abruptly.

    d about unfamiliar topics.

6. When people <u>demean</u> themselves they

    a cause others to disrespect them.

    b get ready to face a challenge.

    c brag about their accomplishments.

    d think they are better than other people.

7. To <u>evoke</u> a response means to

    a expect a response.

    b produce a response.

    c hope for a response.

    d reject a response.

8. I was in <u>excruciating</u> pain after I fell and broke my leg. The pain was

    a mild.

    b due to an accident.

    c extreme.

    d bearable.

9. To <u>inaugurate</u> someone is to

    a elect that person to office in a landslide victory.

    b install that person in office in a formal ceremony.

    c ask that person to run for office.

    d invite that person to a dinner party at the White House.

10. The movie's music and costumes are <u>evocative</u> of London in the 1960s. This means that the music and costumes

    a were created in London during the 1960s.

    b were probably not created in London during the 1960s.

    c are very different from those of 1960s London.

    d help viewers imagine London during the 1960s.

11. When soldiers <u>rebuff</u> an attack they

    a call off the attack.

    b drive their enemy back.

    c declare an end to the war.

    d flee from their enemy.

12. Merriment <u>pervades</u> our town during the holidays. To <u>pervade</u> means to

    a   light up.

    b   appear in some parts.

    c   interrupt.

    d   spread throughout.

13. Rosemary has been through some hard times, but she is <u>resilient</u> enough to

    a   recover and move on with her life.

    b   feel very depressed for a long time.

    c   feel very angry with those who caused her troubles.

    d   understand other people's pain.

14. Where would you be likely to encounter air <u>turbulence</u>?

    a   in a hotel

    b   in a classroom

    c   on an airline flight

    d   in a large auditorium

15. Which of these is MOST <u>resilient</u> after you stretch it?

    a   modeling clay

    b   a cotton sock

    c   a rubber band

    d   a piece of paper

16. What is an <u>inauguration</u>?

    a   a formal installation ceremony

    b   a formal political announcement

    c   the end of a person's political career

    d   a formal dance for the president of the United States

17. Which describes a period of <u>turbulence</u>?

    a   an uneventful time

    b   a time when people make great progress

    c   a long-ago time

    d   a time of great disturbance

18. Which of these might lose its <u>resilience</u>?

    a   a hair elastic that has been used too many times

    b   a boulder sitting in a rushing river

    c   an image on a computer screen

    d   a set of dishes that has been washed many times

Find a SYNONYM for each underlined word. Circle the letter of your answer.

19. The Civil War was a <u>turbulent</u> time in United States history.

    a   chaotic

    b   glorious

    c   fascinating

    d   triumphant

20. The ballet student tried to <u>emulate</u> famous ballerinas like Suzanne Farrell.

    a   praise

    b   criticize

    c   imitate

    d   contact

21. The sergeant's <u>brusque</u> orders made the soldier nervous.

    a   many

    b   insulting

    c   casual

    d   gruff

22. When Aaron asked her to the party, Melissa <u>rebuffed</u> his invitation.

    a   considered

    b   questioned

    c   overlooked

    d   rejected

23. Who is the <u>proprietor</u> of the new store at Oak Square?

    a   owner

    b   clerk

    c   supplier

    d   employee

24. Author Mary Ann Evans's <u>pseudonym</u> was George Eliot.

    a husband

    b pen name

    c nephew

    d nickname

25. It is <u>demeaning</u> to have to beg for an invitation.

    a courageous

    b degrading

    c silly

    d obnoxious

26. Certain songs <u>evoke</u> Mr. Raymer's college days.

    a recall

    b brighten

    c surpass

    d spoil

Find an ANTONYM for each underlined word. Circle the letter of your answer.

27. Taylor is an <u>avid</u> baseball fan.

    a disinterested

    b hometown

    c longtime

    d unusual

28. Mr. Lu wrote a <u>concise</u> memo.

    a fascinating

    b essential

    c wordy

    d interesting

29. Last month we <u>inaugurated</u> a new school system.

    a organized

    b discussed

    c terminated

    d developed

30. It is <u>despicable</u> to steal people's property.

    a   questionable

    b   honorable

    c   understandable

    d   cowardly

31. The Huge Corporation's offer to buy the Petite Company met with a/an <u>rebuff</u>.

    a   snag

    b   acceptance

    c   evasion

    d   problem

32. The small boat sailed on a <u>turbulent</u> sea.

    a   gray-green

    b   foamy

    c   calm

    d   salty

Book 5, Lesson 2 Test

Choose the BEST way to complete each sentence or answer each question. Circle the letter of your answer.

1. To <u>derive</u> a piece of information is to

   a read about it.

   b write about it.

   c obtain it through reasoning.

   d obtain it from the Internet.

2. To <u>electrify</u> a home is to equip it with

   a a swimming pool.

   b solar heating.

   c gas heating.

   d electricity.

3. A store's <u>inventory</u> is

   a its stock of items on hand.

   b the kinds of items it sells.

   c its location.

   d its staff of employees.

4. A <u>grimace</u> is a facial expression that shows

   a shocked surprise.

   b peaceful contentment.

   c pain, contempt, or disgust.

   d disappointment.

5. An <u>endeavor</u> is a serious

   a discussion.

   b crime.

   c error of judgment.

   d effort to reach a goal.

6. Abrasion is the process of

   a wearing or rubbing away through friction.
   b climbing to a higher elevation.
   c becoming disorganized through lack of leadership.
   d building up layers of soil over time.

7. When a patient suffers from dehydration, his or her body needs

   a exercise.
   b fresh air.
   c food.
   d water.

8. Robin derives enjoyment from exercising. In the sentence, derives means

   a gives others.
   b gets.
   c wishes she could get.
   d does not expect to get.

9. When might someone step gingerly?

   a when dancing to loud music
   b when trying to avoid broken glass
   c when hurrying to catch a bus
   d when strolling happily through the park

10. Which is abrasive?

   a sandpaper
   b clay
   c plastic wrap
   d mashed potatoes

11. The fabric of the couch simulates leather. This means that the fabric

   a is real leather.
   b doesn't look anything like leather.
   c is leather printed with a pattern.
   d is made to look and feel like leather.

Find a SYNONYM for each underlined word. Circle the letter of your answer.

12. abrasive

    a clever

    b commanding

    c harsh

    d strong

13. clad

    a joyous

    b checkered

    c sheltered

    d clothed

14. dehydrated

    a dried

    b roasted

    c boiled

    d fried

15. electrified

    a embarrassed

    b thrilled

    c discouraged

    d irritated

16. endeavored

    a attempted

    b journeyed

    c battled

    d forced

17. gingerly

    a obedient

    b generous

    c cheerful

    d cautious

18. gruesome

    a sneaky

    b horrible

    c slimy

    d huge

19. inventory

    a laboratory

    b group

    c list

    d invention

20. succumb

    a yield

    b approach

    c groom

    d pamper

21. surmised

    a examined

    b supposed

    c smiled

    d surprised

22. succumbed

    a lingered

    b died

    c tumbled

    d exploded

23. simulated

    a hid

    b showed

    c inquired

    d pretended

Find an ANTONYM for each underlined word. Circle the letter of your answer.

24. corroborate

    a disrupt

    b disentangle

    c disprove

    d distrust

25. cursory

    a comfortable

    b polite

    c elegant

    d lengthy

26. simulated

    a genuine

    b valuable

    c shiny

    d beautiful

27. dehydrated

    a plump

    b satisfied

    c strong

    d soaked

Find the words that correctly complete each analogy. Circle the letter of your answer.

28. laceration : cut ::

    a abrasion : bruise

    b abrasion : scrape

    c abrasion : break

    d abrasion : injection

29. inquired : asked ::

   a   <u>inventoried</u> : created

   b   <u>inventoried</u> : listed

   c   <u>inventoried</u> : experimented

   d   <u>inventoried</u> : purchased

30. duplication : copying ::

   a   <u>simulation</u> : flying

   b   <u>simulation</u> : driving

   c   <u>simulation</u> : imitating

   d   <u>simulation</u> : genuine

31. proof : evidence ::

   a   <u>surmise</u> : guess

   b   <u>surmise</u> : declaration

   c   <u>surmise</u> : proposal

   d   <u>surmise</u> : idea

32. scowl : anger ::

   a   <u>grimace</u> : pain

   b   <u>grimace</u> : contentment

   c   <u>grimace</u> : surprise

   d   <u>grimace</u> : shyness

Book 5, Lesson 3 Test

Choose the BEST way to complete each sentence or answer each question. Circle the letter of your answer.

1. To <u>modify</u> a law is to

   a pass it swiftly.
   b obey it reluctantly.
   c make it less severe.
   d disobey it on purpose.

2. A <u>pivot</u> is someone

   a on whom others depend.
   b who plays tricks on others.
   c who seems happy most of the time.
   d whom others dislike or distrust.

3. A <u>generation</u> is the average length of time between

   a the birth of parents and their children.
   b space shuttle launches.
   c the summer and winter Olympics.
   d U.S. presidential elections.

4. The baby boom <u>generation</u> is

   a a kind of preschool or kindergarten.
   b a popular rock-and-roll band of the 1960s.
   c the length of time between the Great Depression and the fall of the Berlin Wall.
   d a large group of people born after World War II ended.

5. The Hurleys want to <u>instill</u> good values in their son. This means that they want

   a to believe that their son has good values.
   b to teach good values to their son little by little.
   c to find out if their son has good values.
   d their son to learn good values in school.

---

6. The same idea <u>recurred</u> to Dan several times this week. This means that

   a several different people had the same idea.

   b Dan kept forgetting his idea.

   c the same idea kept coming into Dan's mind.

   d Dan thought of several solutions to the same problem.

7. There were three <u>generations</u> at the Arroyo family reunion. This means that

   a only three children were there.

   b children, parents, and grandparents were there.

   c aunts, uncles, and pets were there.

   d moms, dads, and kids were there.

8. Which of these has a <u>pivot</u>?

   a a swivel chair

   b a granite boulder

   c a spoon

   d a mountain lion

9. A white cat jumped nimbly onto the garage roof. In this sentence, which word <u>modifies</u> the word *jumped*?

   a nimbly

   b cat

   c white

   d roof

10. *Combustion* means burning. Which describes <u>spontaneous</u> combustion?

    a A woman strikes a match to light a candle flame.

    b A man puts another log on a blazing fire.

    c A boy gathers kindling for a campfire.

    d In a deserted garage, a pile of oily rags bursts into flames.

Find a SYNONYM for each underlined word. Circle the letter of your answer.

11. conjecture

    a   proposal

    b   proof

    c   surmise

    d   fantasy

12. disposition

    a   trait

    b   opinion

    c   excuse

    d   temperament

13. encompass

    a   point

    b   guide

    c   enclose

    d   accompany

14. guile

    a   trickery

    b   contentment

    c   kindness

    d   depression

15. imperative

    a   disapproving

    b   fascinating

    c   elegant

    d   urgent

16. modified

    a   smoothed

    b   changed

    c   modernized

    d   explained

17. <u>pivoted</u>

   a   leaped

   b   danced

   c   turned

   d   somersaulted

18. <u>recurred</u>

   a   growled

   b   repeated

   c   performed

   d   healed

19. <u>disposition</u>

   a   tendency

   b   disposal

   c   display

   d   pose

20. <u>imperative</u>

   a   furious

   b   whiny

   c   commanding

   d   surprised

21. <u>recurrence</u>

   a   instance

   b   outbreak

   c   finale

   d   return

Find an ANTONYM for each underlined word. Circle the letter of your answer.

22. <u>prevalent</u>

   a   rare

   b   costly

   c   sparkling

   d   precious

23. conjectured

    a failed

    b rebelled

    c proved

    d escaped

24. encompassed

    a exported

    b captured

    c extricated

    d excluded

25. extricate

    a praise

    b entangle

    c assist

    d ignore

26. pivotal

    a insignificant

    b silent

    c embarrassed

    d plain

27. spontaneous

    a celebratory

    b rehearsed

    c extraordinary

    d fascinating

Find the words that correctly complete each analogy. Circle the letter of your answer.

28. obedience : rebellion ::

   a   spontaneity : joy

   b   spontaneity : deliberation

   c   spontaneity : excitement

   d   spontaneity : affection

29. medley : music ::

   a   anthology : painting

   b   anthology : dance

   c   anthology : writing

   d   anthology : sculpture

30. modest : humble ::

   a   anonymous : famous

   b   anonymous : author

   c   anonymous : unknown

   d   anonymous : donation

...ng a si reading book to read when you are finished?

...gy comes...m two Greek words: *anthos* and *legein*. What do ...words mean

Anthos mea... "flower" and means *legein* "to gather."

... *Anthos* mea... "gather" and means *legein* "together."

c. *Anthos* means "many" and means *legein* "stories."

Book 5, Lesson 4 Test

Choose the BEST way to complete each sentence or answer each question. Circle the letter of your answer.

1. Melanie's dream <u>haunted</u> her. This means that her dream

   a was about a ghost.

   b visited her every night.

   c took place in a haunted house.

   d stayed in her mind continually.

2. To take something <u>amiss</u> is to

   a carry it with you.

   b take it the wrong way.

   c give it to someone as a gift.

   d take it far away.

3. People said that a spirit <u>haunted</u> the house on the hill. People said that

   a a ghost appeared in the house.

   b visitors frequently came to the house.

   c they could not stop thinking about the house.

   d most of their dreams were about the house.

4. Which is likely to include <u>sage</u>?

   a a sauce

   b a book

   c a game

   d a conversation

5. Which is most likely to express <u>profound</u> ideas?

   a a television commercial

   b a book by a great scholar

   c a street sign

   d instructions for making spaghetti

6. David loved horses so he <u>haunted</u> the local stables. This means that David

   a   was a ghost.

   b   thought about the stables every day.

   c   visited the stables frequently.

   d   dreamed about the stables each night.

Find a SYNONYM for each underlined word. Circle the letter of your answer.

7. <u>abhorred</u>

   a   shivered

   b   excluded

   c   explored

   d   detested

8. <u>affable</u>

   a   pleasant

   b   hilarious

   c   edible

   d   drinkable

9. <u>amiss</u>

   a   strong

   b   feminine

   c   wrong

   d   fancy

10. <u>despondent</u>

   a   watery

   b   repulsive

   c   communicative

   d   discouraged

11. <u>entreated</u>

   a   favored

   b   begged

   c   donated

   d   enjoyed

12. impelled

   a expelled
   b propelled
   c improved
   d imported

13. profound

   a scenic
   b preferred
   c deep
   d mournful

14. recluse

   a pioneer
   b hermit
   c tourist
   d teacher

15. reverberated

   a expanded
   b exploded
   c shouted
   d echoed

16. sage

   a wise
   b flashy
   c delicious
   d plain

17. tremulous

   a dewy
   b quiet
   c shaking
   d sobbing

18. impelled

    a urged

    b distressed

    c wrote

    d informed

Find an ANTONYM for each underlined word. Circle the letter of your answer.

19. abhorrent

    a generous

    b appealing

    c informative

    d patient

20. affability

    a stupidity

    b greed

    c elegance

    d hostility

21. entreaty

    a war

    b command

    c theft

    d strength

22. interminable

    a plain

    b easy

    c free

    d quick

23. <u>irascible</u>

    a kind

    b frail

    c smooth

    d temporary

24. <u>reclusive</u>

    a generous

    b social

    c helpful

    d common

25. <u>tremulous</u>

    a bold

    b boring

    c scenic

    d deep

Find the words that correctly complete each analogy. Circle the letter of your answer.

26. hermit : partygoer ::

    a <u>sage</u> : herb

    b <u>sage</u> : wise

    c <u>sage</u> : wisdom

    d <u>sage</u> : fool

27. chat : friendly ::

    a <u>tirade</u> : lengthy

    b <u>tirade</u> : tedious

    c <u>tirade</u> : sorrowful

    d <u>tirade</u> : angry

Name: _____   Date: _____

Book 5, Lesson 5 Test

Choose the BEST way to complete each sentence or answer each question. Circle the letter of your answer.

1. We <u>embarked</u> on our coast-to-coast trip in Portland, Oregon. In Portland, we

   a   began our journey.

   b   ended our journey.

   c   took a break from our journey.

   d   picked up some extra passengers.

2. Which of these people would most likely be involved in a <u>mutiny</u>?

   a   dogs

   b   tow-truck drivers

   c   sailors

   d   ballet dancers

3. Which of these remarks would be considered <u>audacious</u>?

   a   "Move over! I'm coming through!"

   b   "I think it's going to rain today."

   c   "Could you please pass the salt?"

   d   "Be careful! Those stairs are dangerous."

4. She does <u>conscientious</u> work for various charities in the area. The work she does is

   a   boring and unsatisfactory.

   b   fun and adventurous.

   c   tiring and unimportant.

   d   principled and honest.

5. A <u>prudent</u> decision is

   a   wise.

   b   boring.

   c   cowardly.

   d   studious.

6. Why would a teacher <u>rebuke</u> students?

   a   for getting good grades on an exam
   b   for paying attention during class
   c   for planning a class field trip
   d   for not doing their homework

7. The speaker's comment really <u>rankled</u> me. Her comment made me feel

   a   supportive.
   b   irritated.
   c   confident.
   d   tricked.

8. Which of these could you <u>embark</u>?

   a   a horse
   b   a grocery store
   c   a bicycle
   d   a boat

Find a SYNONYM for each underlined word. Circle the letter of your answer.

9. <u>audacious</u>

   a   healthy
   b   hilarious
   c   daring
   d   spacious

10. <u>confiscated</u>

   a   seized
   b   arrested
   c   chased
   d   examined

11. <u>conscientious</u>

   a   scientific
   b   careful
   c   intelligent
   d   hostile

12. depicted

   a framed

   b colored

   c inspected

   d described

13. inkling

   a stain

   b suspicion

   c problem

   d interest

14. pilfer

   a amuse

   b tickle

   c irritate

   d steal

15. profuse

   a artificial

   b healthy

   c abundant

   d leafy

16. slovenly

   a sweltering

   b sleepy

   c untidy

   d disobedient

17. serene

   a peaceful

   b beautiful

   c smooth

   d green

18. mutinied

    a devoured

    b captured

    c screeched

    d rebelled

Find an ANTONYM for each underlined word. Circle the letter of your answer.

19. lackadaisical

    a clumsy

    b enthusiastic

    c gloomy

    d intelligent

20. profusion

    a silence

    b lack

    c clarity

    d shame

21. prudence

    a enjoyment

    b freedom

    c welcome

    d recklessness

22. rebuke

    a compliment

    b valley

    c favor

    d recovery

23. serenity

    a eagerness

    b nervousness

    c destruction

    d illness

24. <u>audacity</u>

    a   timidity

    b   laziness

    c   boredom

    d   dishonesty

Book 5, Lesson 6 Test

Choose the BEST way to complete each sentence or answer each question. Circle the letter of your answer.

1. Mr. McNeal was <u>arraigned</u> for auto theft. This means that he

   a   faced auto theft charges in court.

   b   certainly stole a car.

   c   went to prison for stealing a car.

   d   did not actually steal.

2. Mr. McNeal's lawyer <u>assimilated</u> new facts about the case. This means that she

   a   tracked down some new facts about Mr. McNeal's case.

   b   analyzed new facts about Mr. McNeal's case and proved them false.

   c   took in new facts and combined them with other facts about the case.

   d   figured out how to use new facts to win Mr. McNeal's case.

3. Talent, skill, and hours of practice <u>conspired</u> to win the game for the Kangaroos. In this sentence, <u>conspired</u> means

   a   schemed.

   b   joined together.

   c   made it difficult.

   d   made it impossible.

4. Who would be most likely to wear <u>shackles</u>?

   a   members of the audience at a play

   b   prisoners

   c   guards

   d   zookeepers

5. Sara's mother <u>interrogated</u> her when she got home late. Sara's mother

   a   asked her many thorough questions.

   b   grounded her.

   c   fixed her a meal.

   d   read her a story.

6. The man was <u>lionized</u> after he rescued the baby from a burning building. The man was

    a   given a medal.

    b   treated like a celebrity.

    c   taken to the hospital.

    d   thanked by the child's parents.

Find a SYNONYM for each underlined word. Circle the letter of your answer.

7. <u>apprehended</u>

    a   chased

    b   accused

    c   charged

    d   arrested

8. <u>bizarre</u>

    a   high-pitched

    b   attractive

    c   unusual

    d   cruel

9. <u>calamity</u>

    a   disaster

    b   rescue

    c   incident

    d   prank

10. <u>conspired</u>

    a   sweated

    b   whispered

    c   plotted

    d   grouped

11. <u>elapsed</u>

    a   galloped

    b   passed

    c   stopped

    d   rushed

12. conspiracy

    a plot

    b meeting

    c outline

    d proposal

13. apprehend

    a analyze

    b understand

    c describe

    d question

Find an ANTONYM for each underlined word. Circle the letter of your answer.

14. sweltered

    a froze

    b lounged

    c shrank

    d strolled

15. anarchy

    a kindness

    b silence

    c discipline

    d generosity

16. calamitous

    a flat

    b fortunate

    c attractive

    d timid

17. dissension

    a admiration

    b rising

    c harmony

    d sense

18. meticulous

    a haughty

    b abrasive

    c mismatched

    d sloppy

19. shackled

    a frail

    b vulnerable

    c liberated

    d cheerful

Find the words that correctly complete each analogy. Circle the letter of your answer.

20. previous : earlier ::

    a imminent : soon

    b imminent : later

    c imminent : historical

    d imminent : now

21. education : teaching ::

    a interrogation : police

    b interrogation : formality

    c interrogation : questioning

    d interrogation : response

22. prejudice : tolerance ::

    a shackles : prison

    b shackles : handcuffs

    c shackles : oppression

    d shackles : freedom

23. freezing : cold ::

    a sweltering : hot

    b sweltering : weather

    c sweltering : suffering

    d sweltering : sweating

24. blend : crowd ::

   a   <u>assimilate</u> : generation

   b   <u>assimilate</u> : family

   c   <u>assimilate</u> : population

   d   <u>assimilate</u> : university

25. drought : water ::

   a   <u>anarchy</u> : government

   b   <u>anarchy</u> : intelligence

   c   <u>anarchy</u> : courage

   d   <u>anarchy</u> : history

Book 5, Lesson 7 Test

Choose the BEST way to complete each sentence or answer each question. Circle the letter of your answer.

1. Clarice has <u>claustrophobia</u>. She is afraid of

   a   flying.

   b   heights.

   c   reptiles and amphibians.

   d   small, enclosed spaces.

2. To <u>condescend</u> is to behave in

   a   an outgoing and friendly manner.

   b   an offensively superior manner.

   c   a polite but cool manner.

   d   a sarcastic, mocking manner.

3. A <u>contingent</u> plan is one that

   a   is considered successful.

   b   may be carried out.

   c   will not be used.

   d   is considered unsuccessful.

4. Eli received a <u>deluge</u> of e-mail messages. This means that he received

   a   many, many e-mail messages.

   b   two e-mail messages.

   c   no e-mail messages at all.

   d   the usual number of e-mail messages.

5. A <u>fledgling</u> is

   a   a reckless young person.

   b   a hopeful job seeker.

   c   an inexperienced young person.

   d   a hospital patient.

6. When would you expect to hear a <u>fanfare</u>?

   a   when a customer walks into a store

   b   when a king or queen enters a room

   c   when a movie begins

   d   when a doorbell rings

7. The princess would not <u>condescend</u> to live anywhere but her castle. The princess

   a   was forced to live in the castle.

   b   thought that no place but the castle was good enough for her.

   c   would not let anyone else live in the castle.

   d   had another home besides the castle.

Find a SYNONYM for each underlined word. Circle the letter of your answer.

8. <u>condescending</u>

   a   haughty

   b   humble

   c   welcoming

   d   fearful

9. <u>inanity</u>

   a   hunger

   b   foolishness

   c   cowardice

   d   malice

10. <u>colleague</u>

    a   team

    b   fathom

    c   coworker

    d   message

11. <u>contingent</u>

    a   conditional

    b   contented

    c   massive

    d   mountainous

12. <u>daunted</u>

    a   discouraged

    b   haunted

    c   destroyed

    d   shocked

13. <u>deluge</u>

    a   sled

    b   ending

    c   flood

    d   wind

14. <u>dubbed</u>

    a   stupefied

    b   informed

    c   drowned

    d   nicknamed

15. <u>fanfare</u>

    a   display

    b   motion

    c   outcry

    d   complaint

16. <u>fledgling</u>

    a   clumsy

    b   dangerous

    c   untidy

    d   untested

17. <u>inane</u>

    a   insane

    b   silly

    c   unusual

    d   inaudible

18. mettle

a courage

b attractiveness

c kindness

d intelligence

19. replica

a reason

b model

c knickknack

d toy

20. contingent

a battle

b army

c group

d leader

21. daunting

a fatal

b horrifying

c boring

d intimidating

22. deluged

a contacted

b embraced

c overwhelmed

d expelled

Find an ANTONYM for each underlined word. Circle the letter of your answer.

23. dispelled

a eliminated

b healed

c corrected

d welcomed

24. <u>negligible</u>

    a careful

    b overwhelming

    c alert

    d positive

25. <u>protract</u>

    a expand

    b widen

    c endanger

    d shorten

Find the word that correctly completes the analogy. Circle the letter of your answer.

26. puppy : dog ::

    a <u>fledgling</u> : cat

    b <u>fledgling</u> : bird

    c <u>fledgling</u> : fish

    d <u>fledgling</u> : lion

Book 5, Lesson 8 Test

Choose the BEST way to complete each sentence or answer each question. Circle the letter of your answer.

1. <u>Banter</u> is light, playful

   a   conversation.

   b   eating.

   c   wrestling.

   d   singing.

2. To <u>deploy</u> troops is to

   a   recruit them into the armed services.

   b   train them for battle.

   c   arrange them in battle positions.

   d   arrange for them to leave the armed services.

3. To <u>grapple</u> with a problem is to

   a   try to deal with it.

   b   discover it.

   c   solve it.

   d   avoid thinking about it.

4. A <u>pang</u> is a sudden

   a   inspiration.

   b   sharp feeling of pain or distress.

   c   change of plans that occurs at the last moment.

   d   hailstorm.

5. The manager <u>deployed</u> three of his best waiters to serve the large party. The manager

   a   put his three best waiters to work serving the party.

   b   introduced his three best waiters to the party.

   c   trained three new waiters for the job.

   d   hired three new waiters the night of the event.

6. Which of these is <u>azure</u>?

    a   a glorious sunset

    b   a cloudless sky

    c   a mountain meadow

    d   a forest of pine trees

Find a SYNONYM for each underlined word. Circle the letter of your answer.

7. <u>adept</u>

    a   imaginative

    b   eager

    c   accustomed

    d   skilled

8. <u>crucial</u>

    a   fatal

    b   vital

    c   terrible

    d   plausible

9. <u>fastidious</u>

    a   hungry

    b   swift

    c   lucrative

    d   detail-oriented

10. <u>grappled</u>

    a   wrestled

    b   spotted

    c   mauled

    d   devoured

Find an ANTONYM for each underlined word. Circle the letter of your answer.

11. capacious

    a deserted
    b quiet
    c cramped
    d shabby

12. copious

    a generous
    b contrasting
    c polite
    d scanty

13. decelerate

    a mourn
    b harvest
    c descend
    d accelerate

14. facilitated

    a pretended
    b learned
    c impeded
    d failed

15. fastidious

    a sluggish
    b sleepy
    c easygoing
    d courageous

16. fitful

    a steady
    b sane
    c forgiving
    d incompetent

17. <u>preceded</u>

  a halted

  b struggled

  c followed

  d resisted

Find the words that correctly complete each analogy. Circle the letter of your answer.

18. scarlet : apple ::

  a <u>azure</u> : green

  b <u>azure</u> : sea

  c <u>azure</u> : sun

  d <u>azure</u> : soil

19. visible : eyes ::

  a <u>audible</u> : tongue

  b <u>audible</u> : ears

  c <u>audible</u> : nose

  d <u>audible</u> : fingertips

20. scolding : stern ::

  a <u>bantering</u> : bored

  b <u>bantering</u> : furious

  c <u>bantering</u> : complimentary

  d <u>bantering</u> : playful

21. hammer : pounding ::

  a <u>grapple</u> : grasping

  b <u>grapple</u> : sawing

  c <u>grapple</u> : measuring

  d <u>grapple</u> : digging

Name: _____ Date: _____

Book 5, Lesson 9 Test

Choose the BEST way to complete each sentence or answer each question. Circle the letter of your answer.

1. Which of these materials would you be most likely to <u>staple</u>?

   a blankets

   b sheet metal

   c cookies

   d pieces of paper

2. <u>Diversion</u> is the act of turning

   a away unqualified job seekers.

   b aside from what you were doing.

   c problems into solutions.

   d a task over to another person.

3. To <u>abet</u> a criminal is to

   a follow him or her.

   b arrest him or her.

   c assist him or her.

   d report him or her to the police.

4. Which is a <u>staple</u>?

   a a clothespin or paperclip

   b a U-shaped fastener with sharp ends

   c a bottle of glue or paste

   d a pointed pushpin or thumbtack

5. Someone with an <u>agile</u> mind

   a is suspicious of others.

   b can think quickly and easily.

   c is very good at math.

   d has artistic talent.

6. To <u>divert</u> a flood is to

   a turn floodwaters aside.

   b predict that one will occur.

   c warn people that a flood is coming.

   d prepare for the arrival of a flood.

7. A country's <u>staple</u> crop is

   a its most important crop.

   b a crop grown only to export.

   c an exotic crop grown in small quantities

   d a crop grown to make feed for animals.

8. What kind of <u>diversion</u> might be offered at a child's birthday party?

   a a chocolate cake

   b gifts

   c a clown

   d lemonade

Find a SYNONYM for each underlined word. Circle the letter of your answer.

9. <u>agile</u>

   a dangerous

   b reckless

   c conscientious

   d nimble

10. <u>allotted</u>

    a assigned

    b gathered

    c parked

    d excused

11. <u>balmy</u>

    a stormy

    b windy

    c mild

    d sweltering

12. congregate

a rejoice

b duplicate

c socialize

d assemble

13. diverted

a irritated

b distributed

c entertained

d explained

14. humdrum

a boring

b musical

c rhythmic

d soothing

15. memento

a journal

b jacket

c farewell

d souvenir

16. query

a fear

b question

c comment

d idea

17. tumult

a anger

b concert

c race

d uproar

18. <u>tumultuous</u>

  a watery

  b grouchy

  c turbulent

  d rocky

Find an ANTONYM for each underlined word. Circle the letter of your answer.

19. <u>unseemly</u>

  a smooth

  b appropriate

  c shiny

  d generous

20. <u>agility</u>

  a clumsiness

  b kindness

  c embarrassment

  d untidiness

21. <u>influx</u>

  a laziness

  b stillness

  c awkwardness

  d departure

22. <u>intricate</u>

  a ugly

  b silent

  c simple

  d expensive

23. <u>queried</u>

  a comforted

  b protected

  c replied

  d facilitated

24. <u>sporadic</u>

   a flexible

   b regular

   c humble

   d ordinary

Find the words that correctly complete the analogy. Circle the letter of your answer.

25. uncommon : delicacy ::

   a bread : <u>staple</u>

   b toxic : <u>staple</u>

   c prolific : <u>staple</u>

   d basic : <u>staple</u>

Name: _____   Date: _____

Book 5, Lesson 10 Test

Choose the BEST way to complete each sentence or answer each question. Circle the letter of your answer.

1. An <u>atrocity</u> is an act of great

   a cruelty.

   b ignorance.

   c leadership.

   d cleverness.

2. The <u>élite</u> are people who

   a live in apartment buildings.

   b have superior status to others.

   c have graduated from high school.

   d are less fortunate than others.

3. To <u>wreak</u> your anger is to

   a grow even angrier.

   b calmly explain why you are angry.

   c express it.

   d feel ashamed of it.

4. Who is most likely to live under <u>abject</u> conditions?

   a someone who is artistic

   b someone who is living on the street

   c someone who is brilliant

   d someone who is well educated

5. Monya spoke a French <u>dialect</u> with her parents when she was growing up. Monya spoke

   a grammatically perfect French.

   b a mix of French and Spanish.

   c just a few French phrases that she learned from her grandparents.

   d a special form of French with its own grammar, pronunciation, and vocabulary.

Find a SYNONYM for each underlined word. Circle the letter of your answer.

6. wreaked

    a inflicted

    b squeaked

    c stank

    d destroyed

7. abject

    a typical

    b whiny

    c urgent

    d wretched

8. advocated

    a provoked

    b employed

    c defended

    d organized

9. atrocious

    a dishonest

    b cruel

    c incorrect

    d forceful

10. commemorate

    a recite

    b memorize

    c remember

    d depict

11. dire

    a challenging

    b accidental

    c inconvenient

    d desperate

12. flagrant

    a flowery

    b odorous

    c offensive

    d amazing

13. muted

    a invited

    b softened

    c rebelled

    d felt

14. reprisal

    a retaliation

    b repetition

    c award

    d opening

15. turmoil

    a pain

    b anger

    c confusion

    d fury

Find an ANTONYM for each underlined word. Circle the letter of your answer.

16. advocate

    a bystander

    b opponent

    c leader

    d child

17. enhanced

    a joined

    b freed

    c diminished

    d widened

18. <u>languished</u>

    a   flattened

    b   quieted

    c   dehydrated

    d   flourished

19. <u>mute</u>

    a   talkative

    b   eager

    c   thoughtful

    d   cooperative

20. <u>razed</u>

    a   devoured

    b   lowered

    c   toiled

    d   rebuilt

Find the words that correctly complete each analogy. Circle the letter of your answer.

21. excellent : good ::

    a   <u>atrocious</u> : deed

    b   <u>atrocious</u> : bad

    c   <u>atrocious</u> : unusual

    d   <u>atrocious</u> : appalling

22. wealthy : poor ::

    a   <u>élite</u> : fancy

    b   <u>élite</u> : humble

    c   <u>élite</u> : superior

    d   <u>élite</u> : force

Book 5, Midterm Test 1 (Lessons 1–10)

Read the passage. Choose the BEST answer for each sentence or question about an underlined word. Circle the letter of your answer.

CINDERELLA

adapted from the fairy tale by Charles Perrault

Once upon a time there was a wealthy couple with a wonderful young daughter. Sadly, the girl's mother died. After several years had <u>elapsed</u>, her father remarried. His second wife was a widow with two daughters. All three women were proud, selfish, and mean-spirited. The gentleman's own daughter had a sweet <u>disposition</u>. Since the girl's charming personality made her stepsisters appear even move vulgar, her stepmother despised her. She put her to work as a household slave, scrubbing pots and tending the fire. Her father would have intervened, but he, too, died soon after his remarriage. In the evenings the poor girl would sit in the chimney corner upon the cinders, so her unkind stepsisters <u>dubbed</u> her Cinderella. Since her mother had taught her to be clean and tidy, Cinderella's <u>slovenly</u> appearance humiliated her. This made it doubly <u>excruciating</u> to be called by the derisive nickname.

One day the king announced a birthday ball for his son. All members of the social <u>élite</u> received invitations. For weeks, Cinderella's stepsisters talked of nothing but gowns and hairstyles. When Cinderella timidly asked whether she was invited, her stepmother sneered that it would be <u>unseemly</u> to bring a dirty, ragged girl to the palace. As the family set off for the ball in their finest clothes, Cinderella felt a <u>pang</u> of loneliness and despair.

As she sat weeping she heard a melodious voice. "Well, my dear, isn't it time you were off to the ball?" There stood a radiant old woman, Cinderella's fairy godmother. The talented fairy quickly transformed a pumpkin into a luxurious coach, six gray mice into dapple-gray horses, a fat white rat into a jolly old coachman, and six slithering lizards into footmen in fine clothes. "Our preparations are complete," the fairy godmother announced.

Poor Cinderella stared down at her rags. She spoke in a <u>tremulous</u> voice, holding back tears. "Dear Godmother, I'm not ungrateful, but I can't go <u>clad</u> in this ragged dress."

"Of course not!" laughed the fairy godmother. She touched the girl lightly with her wand, instantly transforming her rags into a shimmering gold and silver gown. On the girl's feet were sparkling glass slippers.

As Cinderella set off, her fairy godmother cautioned her to leave the palace before midnight. At the stroke of twelve, her coach would become a pumpkin once more, her horses and servants would change back into rodents and reptiles, and her gown would melt into rags.

At the ball, the prince fell in love with Cinderella at first sight. All evening he would dance with no one else. Cinderella had such a wonderful time that she forgot to watch the clock. She was eating supper with the prince when she heard the clock begin to strike twelve. Fleeing down the palace steps, she accidentally stepped out of one of her glass slippers. On the last stroke of midnight, her waiting coach disappeared. There sat a large orange pumpkin surrounded by a little group of mice, lizards, and a fat white rat. In rags once again, the girl ran home in the dark. All she had as a <u>memento</u> of the enchanted evening was the remaining glass slipper.

Months later the family heard a <u>fanfare</u> of trumpets and a loud knock at the door. The prince and his servant were going from house to house, searching for the owner of the glass slipper. Each stepsister tried to wedge her huge foot into the tiny shoe, but to no avail. Finally the servant noticed Cinderella and persuaded her to try the shoe on. Her dainty foot slid easily into the slipper. Shyly Cinderella took from her pocket the slipper's mate and slipped it on her other foot. "At last!" cried the prince, embracing her.

Cinderella and the prince were married and lived happily ever after. The new princess treated her stepmother and stepsisters far better than they deserved by inviting them to the palace once a year for tea.

1. In this story, <u>elapsed</u> means

    a   neglected.

    b   passed by.

    c   journeyed.

    d   expired.

2. Cinderella had a sweet <u>disposition</u>. Which is a SYNONYM for <u>disposition</u>?

    a   voice

    b   temperament

    c   smile

    d   appearance

3. In this story, <u>dubbed</u> means

   a described.

   b gave a title to.

   c gave a nickname to.

   d scrubbed.

4. Cinderella felt humiliated by her own <u>slovenly</u> appearance. Which is an ANTONYM for <u>slovenly</u>?

   a tidy

   b beautiful

   c tasteful

   d everyday

5. Cinderella found her nickname <u>excruciating</u>. She found it

   a physically painful.

   b emotionally painful.

   c friendly.

   d unfair.

6. The <u>élite</u> are people who

   a are kings and queens.

   b are talkative and pleasant at parties.

   c live in a certain kingdom.

   d enjoy superior status to others.

7. Cinderella's stepmother said it would be <u>unseemly</u> for the girl to attend the ball. Which is a SYNONYM for <u>unseemly</u>?

   a inconvenient

   b unnecessary

   c inappropriate

   d overwhelming

8. A <u>pang</u> is a

   a hope.

   b dream.

   c sudden painful feeling.

   d sudden decision to fight.

9. Cinderella spoke to her godmother in a <u>tremulous</u> voice. Which is a SYNONYM for <u>tremulous</u>?

   a trembling

   b joyful

   c hopeful

   d disappointed

10. Cinderella was <u>clad</u> in rags. Which is a SYNONYM for <u>clad</u>?

   a dressed

   b humiliated

   c covered

   d shivering

11. Cinderella kept a glass slipper as a <u>memento</u>. Which is a SYNONYM for <u>memento</u>?

   a decoration

   b souvenir

   c safeguard

   d talisman

12. What does <u>fanfare</u> mean in this story?

   a any showy display

   b a large fan carried at a ball

   c a sounding of trumpets

   d a drum roll

Name: _____   Date: _____

Book 5, Midterm Test 2 (Lessons 1–10)

Read the passage. Choose the BEST answer for each sentence or question about an under-lined word. Circle the letter of your answer.

MOUNT ST. HELENS

Up until the spring of 1980, Washington's vast Mount St. Helens wilderness area was a lovely place to visit. Although the mountain was an active volcano, more than a century had passed since its last eruption. For <u>generations</u> the region had been home to many kinds of plants and animals. Mount St. Helens and the Spirit Lake Basin provided recreation for thousands of visitors.

The mountain began to show signs of volcanic unrest in March of that year. The first scientists who came to investigate had an <u>inkling</u> that something big was about to happen. Soon teams of volcanologists (scientists who study volcanoes) were <u>deployed</u> all around the area. They took <u>meticulous</u> measurements of earthquakes, escaping steam, and other signs of volcanic activity deep inside the mountain. Many warned that a <u>calamity</u> was coming. Soon local authorities began to <u>entreat</u> nearby residents to evacuate. The authorities <u>endeavored</u> to get everyone out of the danger zone, but some residents chose to remain.

One of those who wouldn't budge was an old man named Harry Truman. He had the same name as the U.S. President who served at the end of World War II. The Harry on Mount St. Helens became famous for stubbornly refusing to leave his beloved lodge on the mountain. Throughout the spring of 1980, scientists warned him that a major eruption was <u>imminent</u>, but Harry stayed put.

By mid-May, earthquakes shook the mountain almost daily. Plumes of gas, smoke, and ash rose ominously into the Washington sky. Hundreds of scientists and a fascinated nation watched and waited. Then on the morning of May 18, 1980, Mount St. Helens erupted. The north face of the mountain collapsed in a massive explosion. In a few moments, a gigantic slab of rock and ice slammed into nearby Spirit Lake. A <u>deluge</u> of debris roared fourteen miles down the Toutle River.

Next, a tremendous second explosion swept over ridges and toppled trees. The blast devastated nearly 150 square miles of forest. At the same time, a mushroom-shaped column of ash rose thousands of feet into the air, turning day into night. Gray ash fell all across western Washington and beyond. Tons of rock and mud scoured the volcano's sides. The eruption lasted nine hours, <u>wreaking</u> terrible damage.

Fifty-seven people died on Mount St. Helens that day. Among them were many dedicated scientists and <u>irascible</u> Harry Truman. In time, nature proved remarkably <u>resilient</u>. Surviving plants and animals rose out of the ash, reestablishing life. In 1982 Congress created the National Volcanic Monument. This is a 110,000-acre park and research area near Mount St. Helens. Thousands of visitors come to view the volcano each year. Today Mount St. Helens remains an awesome reminder of nature's power.

1. Read this sentence from the passage.

For <u>generations</u> the region had been home to many kinds of plants and animals.

In this sentence, <u>generations</u> means

   a   parents and grandparents.

   b   spans of time.

   c   people born around the same time.

   d   animals born around the same time.

2. Read this sentence from the passage.

The first scientists who came to investigate had an <u>inkling</u> that something big was about to happen.

In this sentence, <u>inkling</u> means

   a   suspicion.

   b   message.

   c   warning.

   d   proof.

3. Read these words from the passage.

Soon teams of volcanologists . . . were <u>deployed</u> all around the area.

In this sentence, <u>deployed</u> means

   a   getting ready for battle.

   b   hiking.

   c   put to work.

   d   conducting experiments.

4. Read these words from the passage.

They took <u>meticulous</u> measurements of . . . signs of volcanic activity deep inside the mountain.

<u>Meticulous</u> measurements are

    a   unnecessary.

    b   urgent.

    c   extremely careful.

    d   made by doctors.

5. Read this sentence from the passage.

Many warned that a <u>calamity</u> was coming.

In this sentence, <u>calamity</u> means

    a   snowstorm.

    b   spring flood.

    c   volcano.

    d   disaster.

6. Read this sentence from the passage.

Soon local authorities began to <u>entreat</u> nearby residents to evacuate.

In this sentence, <u>entreat</u> means

    a   plead with.

    b   order.

    c   transport.

    d   make plans for.

7. Read this sentence from the passage.

The authorities <u>endeavored</u> to get everyone out of the danger zone, but some residents chose to remain.

In this sentence, <u>endeavored</u> means

    a   hoped.

    b   made a serious effort.

    c   made a reckless attempt.

    d   forced.

8. Read these words from the passage.

Throughout the spring of 1980, scientists warned him that a major eruption was <u>imminent</u> . . .

In this sentence, <u>imminent</u> means

- **a**   possible.
- **b**   extremely dangerous.
- **c**   about to happen.
- **d**   fatal.

9. Read this sentence from the passage.

A <u>deluge</u> of debris roared fourteen miles down the Toutle River.

In this sentence, <u>deluge</u> means

- **a**   flood.
- **b**   lake.
- **c**   rainfall.
- **d**   pile.

10. Read this sentence from the passage.

The eruption lasted nine hours, <u>wreaking</u> terrible damage.

In this sentence, <u>wreaking</u> means

- **a**   witnessing.
- **b**   inflicting.
- **c**   describing.
- **d**   uncovering.

11. Read this sentence from the passage.

Among them were many dedicated scientists and <u>irascible</u> Harry Truman.

In this sentence, <u>irascible</u> means

- **a**   frail.
- **b**   courageous.
- **c**   loyal.
- **d**   irritable.

12. Read this sentence from the passage.

In time, nature proved remarkably <u>resilient</u>.

In this sentence, <u>resilient</u> means that nature

    a   has a remarkable ability to recover.

    b   can be remarkably terrifying.

    c   is remarkably beautiful.

    d   is remarkably cruel.

Name: _____   Date: _____

Book 5, Lesson 11 Test

Choose the BEST way to complete each sentence or answer each question. Circle the letter of your answer.

1. To <u>execute</u> an artwork is to

   a buy it.

   b sell it.

   c create it.

   d destroy it.

2. A <u>connoisseur</u> of fine food

   a owns many kitchen tools.

   b is a professional chef.

   c has extensive knowledge of food and cooking.

   d owns a restaurant.

3. Janet <u>discerned</u> her mother's handwriting on the envelope. This means that she

   a looked for her mother's handwriting but could not find it.

   b recognized her mother's handwriting, since it was different from other people's.

   c tried to read her mother's handwriting.

   d thought the handwriting might be her mother's, but wasn't quite sure.

4. When he tells stories, Eli tends to <u>embellish</u> the truth. This means that he

   a avoids lying.

   b adds factual details to his stories.

   c adds made-up details to his stories.

   d sometimes lies to protect himself.

5. *Little Women* <u>exemplifies</u> Louisa May Alcott's best work. This means that the novel

   a is not among Alcott's best works.

   b shows what Alcott's best work is like.

   c is better than anything else Alcott wrote.

   d proves that Alcott is among America's best novelists.

6. Some criminals use stolen identification cards to <u>impersonate</u> their victims. This means that the criminals

   a confuse their victims.

   b embarrass their victims.

   c steal money from their victims.

   d pretend to be their victims.

7. Who has a <u>pastoral</u> occupation?

   a a minister

   b a shepherd

   c a businessperson

   d a gardener

8. To <u>execute</u> a task is to

   a carry it out.

   b ask someone else to do it.

   c do it later.

   d refuse to do it.

Find a SYNONYM for each underlined word. Circle the letter of your answer.

9. <u>benign</u>

   a courageous

   b neglectful

   c close

   d gentle

10. <u>discerned</u>

   a described

   b sympathized

   c comprehended

   d explained

11. embellished

    a decorated

    b exploded

    c constructed

    d devoured

12. grotesque

    a graceful

    b bizarre

    c rocky

    d unruly

13. hallowed

    a celebratory

    b costumed

    c sacred

    d grim

14. impersonated

    a stole

    b recognized

    c criticized

    d mimicked

15. malevolence

    a violence

    b courage

    c hatred

    d strength

16. renown

    a wealth

    b influence

    c power

    d fame

17. <u>discerning</u>

    a kindly

    b jolly

    c perceptive

    d humble

Find an ANTONYM for each underlined word. Circle the letter of your answer.

18. <u>augment</u>

    a reduce

    b dishonor

    c lend

    d teach

19. <u>benign</u>

    a small

    b harmful

    c vain

    d strict

20. <u>discerned</u>

    a praised

    b concealed

    c falsified

    d overlooked

21. <u>malevolent</u>

    a quiet

    b loving

    c serene

    d nonviolent

22. <u>ornate</u>

    a simple

    b comfortable

    c welcoming

    d dilapidated

23. <u>precarious</u>

    a ordinary

    b reclusive

    c plain

    d secure

24. <u>renowned</u>

    a frail

    b unknown

    c untalented

    d unattractive

Find the words that correctly complete each analogy. Circle the letter of your answer.

25. apprehend : capture ::

    a <u>execute</u> : kill

    b <u>execute</u> : imprison

    c <u>execute</u> : scold

    d <u>execute</u> : warn

26. urban : city ::

    a <u>pastoral</u> : simple

    b <u>pastoral</u> : charming

    c <u>pastoral</u> : country

    d <u>pastoral</u> : shepherd

Book 5, Lesson 12 Test

Choose the BEST way to complete each sentence or answer each question. Circle the letter of your answer.

1. Anne was <u>immersed</u> in an art project. This means that the project

   a was extremely difficult.

   b took her full attention.

   c did not interest her very much.

   d was a painting of the ocean.

2. A <u>panorama</u> is a thorough

   a presentation of a subject.

   b knowledge of cooking.

   c grasp of a language.

   d familiarity with a country's culture.

3. Words such as *etiquette* and *gourmet* that we use in English are <u>legacies</u> of the French language. This means that these words

   a are no longer part of the French language.

   b passed into the English language long ago.

   c were given to English-speaking people as gifts.

   d are not really part of the English language.

4. Stella paid for college with her <u>legacy</u> from her grandfather. In this sentence, <u>legacy</u> means

   a a check.

   b money that her grandfather left her in his will.

   c a loan.

   d money that her grandfather gave her for her birthday.

Find a SYNONYM for each underlined word. Circle the letter of your answer.

5. accede

   a consent

   b succeed

   c confess

   d answer

6. affluent

   a tardy

   b talkative

   c wealthy

   d swift

7. artisan

   a dealer

   b architect

   c craftsperson

   d collector

8. irksome

   a itchy

   b odd

   c gruesome

   d annoying

9. ostentatious

   a showy

   b tasty

   c artificial

   d expensive

10. prestigious

   a first

   b esteemed

   c wealthy

   d extravagant

11. reticence

    a embarrassment

    b annoyance

    c vanity

    d silence

12. arbitrary

    a capricious

    b judgmental

    c nervous

    d fair

13. prestige

    a honor

    b leadership

    c intelligence

    d bravery

Find an ANTONYM for each underlined word. Circle the letter of your answer.

14. reticent

    a massive

    b generous

    c talkative

    d plentiful

15. affluence

    a silence

    b misery

    c disrepair

    d poverty

16. dismantle

    a dress

    b hide

    c assemble

    d lie

17. philanthropy

    a   vanity

    b   stinginess

    c   envy

    d   disobedience

Find the words that correctly complete each analogy. Circle the letter of your answer.

18. star : actor ::

    a   tycoon : businessperson

    b   tycoon : famous

    c   tycoon : teacher

    d   tycoon : powerful

19. turbulent : chaotic ::

    a   prolific : generous

    b   prolific : productive

    c   prolific : writer

    d   prolific : produce

20. miser : saving ::

    a   philanthropist : donation

    b   philanthropist : teaching

    c   philanthropist : wealthy

    d   philanthropist : giving

21. banquet : snack ::

    a   panorama : sound

    b   panorama : glimpse

    c   panorama : window

    d   panorama : ocean

22. bury : soil ::

    a   immerse : gravel

    b   immerse : liquid

    c   immerse : dehydrate

    d   immerse : sand

Name: _____   Date: _____

Book 5, Lesson 13 Test

Choose the BEST way to complete each sentence or answer each question. Circle the letter of your answer.

1. To <u>chaperone</u> a school event is to

   a   make sure younger people behave well at the event.

   b   organize the event.

   c   buy a ticket for that event.

   d   make sure everyone has a good time at the event.

2. To <u>contemplate</u> a change is to

   a   hope that things will change.

   b   wonder whether things will ever change.

   c   resist changing.

   d   intend to change.

3. To <u>wrangle</u> a loan is to

   a   repay a loan.

   b   obtain a loan by arguing.

   c   refuse to give someone a loan.

   d   arrange a loan for someone.

4. Which of these would be a <u>deterrent</u> to going to watch a ball game at a local park?

   a   a gentle breeze

   b   warm, sunny weather

   c   pouring rain

   d   getting a good grade in science

5. Wei has a real <u>flair</u> for painting. This means that she

   a   is better at sculpting.

   b   is a very talented painter.

   c   would rather play hockey than paint.

   d   has taken many art classes.

6. Which of these is an <u>integral</u> part of a car?

   a power windows

   b a radio

   c four doors

   d an engine

7. Mr. Tucker's <u>ardent</u> argument for the new library helped to get the necessary funding. Mr. Tucker's argument was

   a sparkling.

   b fragrant.

   c exquisite.

   d passionate.

8. The <u>vivacious</u> counselor made the campers feel welcome right away. The counselor was

   a lively and spirited.

   b bossy and overbearing.

   c shy and reserved.

   d calm and soothing.

Find a SYNONYM for each underlined word. Circle the letter of your answer.

9. <u>ardor</u>

   a anger

   b garden

   c fragrance

   d passion

10. <u>contemplate</u>

   a ponder

   b copy

   c organize

   d serve

11. innovative

    a esteemed

    b original

    c exquisite

    d famous

12. vivacity

    a kindness

    b nervousness

    c liveliness

    d generosity

13. wrangled

    a shouted

    b strangled

    c dangled

    d argued

14. intellect

    a greed

    b vanity

    c malice

    d intelligence

Find an ANTONYM for each underlined word. Circle the letter of your answer.

15. brevity

    a length

    b laughter

    c lightness

    d fascination

16. deter

    a soothe

    b facilitate

    c reveal

    d precede

17. <u>risqué</u>

    a   kind

    b   plain

    c   proper

    d   boring

18. <u>stymied</u>

    a   ascended

    b   assembled

    c   aided

    d   controlled

19. <u>intellect</u>

    a   lawyer

    b   miser

    c   seller

    d   fool

Find the words that correctly complete each analogy. Circle the letter of your answer.

20. glancing : shy ::

    a   <u>ogling</u> : timid

    b   <u>ogling</u> : bold

    c   <u>ogling</u> : illegal

    d   <u>ogling</u> : careful

21. custom : old ::

    a   <u>innovation</u> : new

    b   <u>innovation</u> : conventional

    c   <u>innovation</u> : cultural

    d   <u>innovation</u> : method

22. police officer : law-abiding ::

    a   <u>chaperone</u> : teenagers

    b   <u>chaperone</u> : supervising

    c   <u>chaperone</u> : dancing

    d   <u>chaperone</u> : well-behaved

23. inventory : store ::

a <u>agenda</u> : list

b <u>agenda</u> : purchase

c <u>agenda</u> : meeting

d <u>agenda</u> : item

Book 5, Lesson 14 Test

Choose the BEST way to complete each sentence or answer each question. Circle the letter of your answer.

1. The clock next to my bed has a <u>luminous</u> dial. This means that the dial

   a   gives off light.
   b   is round.
   c   has a second hand.
   d   uses Roman numerals.

2. The concert in the park was <u>sublime</u>. The concert was

   a   acceptable.
   b   splendid.
   c   green.
   d   thoughtful.

3. Which of these might you <u>dissect</u> in biology?

   a   a test tube
   b   a frog
   c   a pencil
   d   water

4. The low water levels made the river <u>stagnant</u>. This means that the river was

   a   dirty.
   b   filled with debris.
   c   not moving.
   d   flowing at a slower pace than usual.

Find a SYNONYM for each underlined word. Circle the letter of your answer.

5. congenial

   a experimental

   b congealed

   c mixed

   d agreeable

6. deciphered

   a spelled

   b wondered

   c decoded

   d puzzled

7. dissected

   a distributed

   b battled

   c infected

   d analyzed

8. enigma

   a symbol

   b letter

   c mystery

   d lava

9. mired

   a stuck

   b injured

   c furious

   d irritated

10. vie

   a change

   b win

   c experiment

   d compete

11. enigmatic

    a   puzzling

    b   automatic

    c   energetic

    d   unimportant

Find an ANTONYM for each underlined word. Circle the letter of your answer.

12. congenial

    a   watery

    b   irascible

    c   separate

    d   worried

13. ineffectual

    a   related

    b   monotonous

    c   starving

    d   successful

14. infallible

    a   frail

    b   unreliable

    c   joyful

    d   honest

15. luminous

    a   unclear

    b   bright

    c   cold

    d   short

16. stagnated

    a   tiptoed

    b   welcomed

    c   flourished

    d   comforted

17. voluminous

    a insufficient

    b secretive

    c impolite

    d dark

18. irrepressible

    a honorable

    b timid

    c smooth

    d correct

Find the words that correctly complete each analogy. Circle the letter of your answer.

19. catastrophe : misfortune ::

    a pestilence : sick

    b pestilence : insecticide

    c pestilence : annoying

    d pestilence : disease

20. beach : sand ::

    a mire : ocean

    b mire : mud

    c mire : desert

    d mire : trees

21. century : 100 ::

    a millennium : 1

    b millennium : 10

    c millennium : 1,000

    d millennium : 10,000

22. steadfast : loyal ::

    a infallible : error

    b infallible : correct

    c infallible : always

    d infallible : flawed

23. organize : messy ::

   a   <u>decipher</u> : disrespectful

   b   <u>decipher</u> : impolite

   c   <u>decipher</u> : illegal

   d   <u>decipher</u> : puzzling

Book 5, Lesson 15 Test

Choose the BEST way to complete each sentence or answer each question. Circle the letter of your answer.

1. To <u>discredit</u> a theory is to

    a   persuade people to investigate it.

    b   prove it.

    c   invent it.

    d   destroy people's confidence in it.

2. Which might make a <u>lurid</u> glow?

    a   a streetlight on a clear night

    b   a sunrise on a clear morning

    c   a sunset on a hazy evening

    d   a bedside lamp

3. To whom is a teacher most likely to show <u>deference</u>?

    a   students who earn high grades

    b   students who sometimes fail to turn in their homework

    c   disrespectful students

    d   the school principal

4. Why might a gardener <u>cull</u> her vegetable garden?

    a   to make sure her plants have enough water

    b   to remove weeds

    c   to fertilize the soil in her garden

    d   because it is time to harvest her vegetables

5. Shane felt a sense of <u>foreboding</u> when he entered the haunted house at the carnival. Shane felt

    a   frightened but excited.

    b   like something bad was going to happen.

    c   like the decorations didn't seem very authentic.

    d   sick and shaky.

6. The park was under police <u>surveillance</u> during the outdoor music festival. The police were

    a   checking in occasionally during the event.

    b   stationed at checkpoints around the park.

    c   working at the information booth.

    d   watching the park carefully.

Find a SYNONYM for each underlined word. Circle the letter of your answer.

7. <u>ascertain</u>

    a   protect

    b   explain

    c   determine

    d   organize

8. <u>chastise</u>

    a   rebuke

    b   silence

    c   instruct

    d   counsel

9. <u>defer</u>

    a   plan

    b   scheme

    c   finalize

    d   postpone

10. <u>desist</u>

    a   sicken

    b   stop

    c   insist

    d   discourage

11. <u>lurid</u>

    a   irritating

    b   uncomfortable

    c   gruesome

    d   depressing

Find an ANTONYM for each underlined word. Circle the letter of your answer.

12. <u>irrational</u>

    a   tolerant

    b   welcoming

    c   generous

    d   sensible

13. <u>humane</u>

    a   cruel

    b   childish

    c   disobedient

    d   unimportant

14. <u>restive</u>

    a   mournful

    b   patient

    c   exhausted

    d   friendly

15. <u>stamina</u>

    a   lightheartedness

    b   brevity

    c   courage

    d   weakness

16. <u>chastised</u>

    a   lectured

    b   praised

    c   warned

    d   avoided

Find the words that correctly complete each analogy. Circle the letter of your answer.

17. overflow : container ::

    a <u>encroach</u> : advance

    b <u>encroach</u> : attack

    c <u>encroach</u> : boundary

    d <u>encroach</u> : army

18. shame : self-esteem ::

    a <u>discredit</u> : evildoer

    b <u>discredit</u> : accuse

    c <u>discredit</u> : hurt

    d <u>discredit</u> : reputation

19. mock : disrespect ::

    a <u>defer</u> : knowledge

    b <u>defer</u> : respect

    c <u>defer</u> : authority

    d <u>defer</u> : ruler

20. praise : criticize ::

    a <u>perpetuate</u> : terminate

    b <u>perpetuate</u> : indefinite

    c <u>perpetuate</u> : continue

    d <u>perpetuate</u> : facilitate

Name: _____   Date: _____

Book 5, Lesson 16 Test

Choose the BEST way to complete each sentence or answer each question. Circle the letter of your answer.

1. A <u>pungent</u> smell is a

   a sweet fragrance.
   b sharp smell.
   c spicy odor.
   d flowery scent.

2. To <u>indulge</u> your love for junk food is to

   a allow yourself to eat junk food.
   b eat healthier foods.
   c insist that junk food is delicious.
   d find out how much fat junk food contains.

3. Which is an <u>antidote</u> to boredom?

   a tedious chores
   b an interesting activity
   c dull weather
   d sleepy people

4. What might a doctor tell you to do to <u>alleviate</u> a headache?

   a take aspirin
   b listen to loud music
   c do homework
   d run a marathon

5. A week after the party, the flowers <u>lolled</u> in the vase. The flowers were

   a still standing up straight.
   b drooping.
   c dried out.
   d faded and lifeless.

Find a SYNONYM for each underlined word. Circle the letter of your answer.

6. bedlam

   a   bedtime

   b   celebration

   c   exhaustion

   d   confusion

7. cajole

   a   cheer

   b   capture

   c   coax

   d   entertain

8. haggard

   a   exhausted

   b   ancient

   c   untidy

   d   filthy

9. incessant

   a   unpleasant

   b   continual

   c   impolite

   d   uncomfortable

10. indulge

    a   punish

    b   control

    c   push

    d   spoil

11. lolled

    a   rolled

    b   slept

    c   sprawled

    d   bounced

12. pungent

    a neutral

    b thoughtful

    c critical

    d careful

13. rue

    a accept

    b dread

    c remember

    d regret

14. strident

    a shrill

    b confident

    c commanding

    d grave

15. immaculate

    a silent

    b flawless

    c pale

    d hungry

Find an ANTONYM for each underlined word. Circle the letter of your answer.

16. vehement

    a mild

    b defeated

    c generous

    d humane

17. glib

    a tiny

    b inflexible

    c sincere

    d imprisoned

18. immaculate

a full

b noisy

c patient

d filthy

19. indulgent

a thin

b reticent

c strict

d serious

Find the words that correctly complete each analogy. Circle the letter of your answer.

20. pebble : boulder ::

a pittance : income

b pittance : purse

c pittance : fortune

d pittance : accounting

21. disease : cure ::

a dangerous : antidote

b poison : antidote

c relieve : antidote

d remedy : antidote

Name: _____   Date: _____

Book 5, Lesson 17 Test

Choose the BEST way to complete each sentence or answer each question. Circle the letter of your answer.

1. A <u>coup</u> is an action that brings

   a prosperity.

   b suffering.

   c major change.

   d joy to all.

2. Ms. McIlvaine <u>bequeathed</u> her love of writing to us. This means that Ms. McIlvaine

   a told us that she loves to write.

   b wrote to us.

   c died.

   d passed her love of writing on to us.

3. An <u>institute</u> is an organization that

   a provides housing for international tourists.

   b cares for people who are mentally ill.

   c promotes education or another cause.

   d governs a nation.

4. The governor's speech was more than just <u>rhetoric</u>. In the sentence, <u>rhetoric</u> means

   a the art of using language skillfully.

   b exaggerated or insincere language.

   c the art of teaching children how to speak properly.

   d language that is difficult to understand.

5. Which of these describes a <u>patriarch</u>?

   a the female head of a family

   b the male head of a family

   c the oldest male employee in a company

   d the female principal of a school

6. In a military <u>coup</u>, soldiers

    a   strengthen the existing government.

    b   elect new government leaders.

    c   overthrow the existing government.

    d   protect a nation from invasion.

Find a SYNONYM for each underlined word. Circle the letter of your answer.

7. <u>accord</u>

    a   comprehension

    b   music

    c   rope

    d   agreement

8. <u>bequest</u>

    a   legacy

    b   journey

    c   desire

    d   goal

9. <u>citadel</u>

    a   tower

    b   church

    c   fortress

    d   bell

10. <u>conferred</u>

    a   delayed

    b   bestowed

    c   transported

    d   covered

11. <u>epoch</u>

    a   achievement

    b   year

    c   novel

    d   era

12. <u>instituted</u>

    a established

    b punished

    c argued

    d instructed

13. <u>rapport</u>

    a proposal

    b harmony

    c essay

    d comment

14. <u>renounce</u>

    a pronounce

    b reject

    c proclaim

    d avoid

15. <u>confer</u>

    a consult

    b lengthen

    c facilitate

    d agree

Find an ANTONYM for each underlined word. Circle the letter of your answer.

16. <u>affirm</u>

    a pretend

    b liquefy

    c deny

    d flee

17. <u>impeccable</u>

    a faulty

    b frail

    c kindly

    d noisy

18. renunciation

    a silence
    b boldness
    c acceptance
    d profusion

Find the words that correctly complete each analogy. Circle the letter of your answer.

19. dance : movement ::

    a rhetoric : building
    b rhetoric : language
    c rhetoric : drawing
    d rhetoric : sculpture

20. involved : conversation ::

    a embroiled : friendship
    b embroiled : correspondence
    c embroiled : chat
    d embroiled : argument

21. president : leadership ::

    a dignitary : membership
    b dignitary : humility
    c dignitary : honor
    d dignitary : unity

22. give : gift ::

    a bequeath : promotion
    b bequeath : vacation
    c bequeath : inheritance
    d bequeath : deceased

Book 5, Lesson 18 Test

Choose the BEST way to complete each sentence or answer each question. Circle the letter of your answer.

1. The community members decided to turn the unused <u>tract</u> into a park. In this sentence, <u>tract</u> means

   a parking lot.
   b building.
   c classroom.
   d area of land.

2. The eighth grade needs to vote on a new <u>delegate</u> to the student council. A <u>delegate</u> is a

   a representative.
   b president.
   c member.
   d chairperson.

3. You should not put <u>combustible</u> materials near

   a a fire.
   b water.
   c a garden.
   d garbage cans.

4. The <u>inclement</u> weather made it difficult for us to enjoy our vacation. The weather was

   a sunny.
   b stormy.
   c humid.
   d warm.

5. I enjoyed reading the movie star's <u>memoir</u>. I enjoyed reading her

   a acceptance speech from an awards ceremony.
   b interview with her costar.
   c list of recommended exercise routines.
   d stories of personal experience.

6. Which of these is a <u>tract</u>?

   a   your digestive system

   b   your spine

   c   your left foot

   d   your eyes, nose, ears, and mouth

Find a SYNONYM for each underlined word. Circle the letter of your answer.

7. <u>aperture</u>

   a   opening

   b   eye

   c   twig

   d   fruit

8. <u>cache</u>

   a   cave

   b   coin

   c   hoard

   d   value

9. <u>delegated</u>

   a   created

   b   entered

   c   described

   d   assigned

10. <u>malady</u>

    a   midwife

    b   tune

    c   illness

    d   sarcasm

11. <u>rectified</u>

    a   reprimanded

    b   commanded

    c   corrected

    d   chastised

12. tribulation

    a   quaking

    b   suffering

    c   praising

    d   reporting

13. requisite

    a   requirement

    b   skill

    c   talent

    d   knowledge

14. tract

    a   drawing

    b   outline

    c   pamphlet

    d   diagram

Find an ANTONYM for each underlined word. Circle the letter of your answer.

15. inclement

    a   careful

    b   merciful

    c   obedient

    d   prompt

16. indelible

    a   readable

    b   sloppy

    c   erasable

    d   elegant

17. requisite

    a   disorganized

    b   preceding

    c   easy

    d   optional

Find the words that correctly complete each analogy. Circle the letter of your answer.

18. frail : ill ::

   a   <u>squeamish</u> : injured

   b   <u>squeamish</u> : nauseated

   c   <u>squeamish</u> : irritated

   d   <u>squeamish</u> : fooled

19. closet : clothing ::

   a   <u>cache</u> : hiding

   b   <u>cache</u> : valuables

   c   <u>cache</u> : containers

   d   <u>cache</u> : storage

20. hungry : ravenous ::

   a   attractive : <u>paramount</u>

   b   curious : <u>paramount</u>

   c   important : <u>paramount</u>

   d   hungry : <u>paramount</u>

21. epic : long ::

   a   <u>vignette</u> : short

   b   <u>vignette</u> : emotional

   c   <u>vignette</u> : mournful

   d   <u>vignette</u> : fitful

Book 5, Lesson 19 Test

Choose the BEST way to complete each sentence or answer each question. Circle the letter of your answer.

1. The festival <u>culminated</u> with a performance by a well-known jazz musician. The musician's performance was

    a   the first concert during the festival.

    b   the final, most important concert of the festival.

    c   a warm-up act for the main performance.

    d   free of charge.

2. A <u>bulwark</u> is a wall-like structure used

    a   to enclose a garden.

    b   for defense or protection.

    c   to muffle sound.

    d   as an animal pen.

3. Albert <u>glutted</u> himself on peanut butter sandwiches. This means that he

    a   had a small snack.

    b   ate much more than he needed to.

    c   ate enough to satisfy his hunger.

    d   ate only one sandwich.

4. Shelby <u>wrested</u> the sweater from her sister's grasp. This means that Shelby

    a   pulled gently on the sweater until her sister gave up.

    b   ripped the sweater as she pulled it.

    c   stretched the sweater as she pulled it.

    d   pulled the sweater away with a twist.

5. Ms. Lopez isn't sure if our science experiment is feasible. Ms. Lopez is worried that our experiment is not

   a   expensive.

   b   worthwhile.

   c   doable.

   d   challenging.

6. Which of these is a natural <u>phenomenon</u>?

   a   a dirt road

   b   a shooting star

   c   the Empire State building

   d   the price of milk

7. The <u>havoc</u> caused by the tornado was difficult to believe. In this sentence, <u>havoc</u> means

   a   winds.

   b   fury.

   c   depression.

   d   devastation.

8. The military <u>wrested</u> control from elected leaders. In this sentence, <u>wrested</u> means

   a   obtained by arguing.

   b   demanded.

   c   requested.

   d   took by force.

9. The camp rules <u>stipulated</u> that the lights be out by 10:00. This means that

   a   10:00 was the suggested time for lights-out.

   b   the lights should be out by sometime between 10:00 and 11:00.

   c   it was a requirement that the lights be off by 10:00.

   d   it didn't matter when the lights were turned off.

Find a SYNONYM for each underlined word. Circle the letter of your answer.

10. <u>culmination</u>

   a   climax

   b   admiration

   c   removal

   d   middle

11. indefatigable

 a talkative
 b slender
 c joyful
 d tireless

12. onslaught

 a attack
 b defeat
 c retreat
 d victory

13. phenomenal

 a holy
 b anonymous
 c extraordinary
 d imaginary

14. engulfed

 a killed
 b injured
 c discouraged
 d overwhelmed

15. bulwark

 a acceptance
 b protection
 c friendship
 d citizenship

Find an ANTONYM for each underlined word. Circle the letter of your answer.

16. glut

 a generosity
 b compliment
 c purity
 d scarcity

17. impregnable

   a vulnerable

   b capable

   c intelligent

   d satisfied

18. phenomenon

   a usual

   b delight

   c expert

   d fool

19. susceptible

   a experienced

   b intelligent

   c protected

   d knowledgeable

20. glutted

   a agreed

   b scoured

   c aided

   d drained

Find the words that correctly complete each analogy. Circle the letter of your answer.

21. identical : appearance ::

   a simultaneous : place

   b simultaneous : time

   c simultaneous : weight

   d simultaneous : color

22. delicious : taste ::

   a picturesque : texture

   b picturesque : sound

   c picturesque : odor

   d picturesque : sight

23. joy : happiness ::

a <u>havoc</u> : boredom

b <u>havoc</u> : curiosity

c <u>havoc</u> : confusion

d <u>havoc</u> : sadness

Name: _____ Date: _____

Book 5, Lesson 20 Test

Choose the BEST way to complete each sentence or answer each question. Circle the letter of your answer.

1. Inflammatory speech makes people

   a feel inspired.
   b angry.
   c remember the past.
   d feel patriotic.

2. An infection inflamed the wound. This means that the wound

   a was healing slowly.
   b required stitches.
   c was sore and swollen.
   d was not serious.

3. Please forbear revealing my secret. In this sentence, forbear means

   a consider.
   b don't worry about.
   c wait a while before.
   d hold back from.

4. Living far away from home sometimes makes me feel alienated from my family. I feel

   a independent and happy.
   b distinguished.
   c alone and cut off from my family.
   d overworked.

5. The poet wrote with such fervor that Shayna couldn't put the book down. In this sentence, fervor means

   a compassion.
   b love.
   c intense feeling.
   d kindness.

6. My friends love to play practical jokes on me because I am so <u>gullible</u>. I am easily

a excited.

b fooled.

c nauseated.

d upset.

Find a SYNONYM for each underlined word. Circle the letter of your answer.

7. <u>hindrance</u>

a distance

b obstacle

c annoyance

d loss

8. <u>inflamed</u>

a challenged

b confused

c angered

d saddened

9. <u>ordained</u>

a disordered

b preached

c explained

d ordered

10. <u>reproached</u>

a angered

b blamed

c proceeded

d considered

11. <u>surpassed</u>

a hurried

b raced

c exceeded

d matched

12. vilified

    a slandered

    b questioned

    c argued

    d pestered

13. rejoinder

    a reply

    b criticism

    c taunt

    d compliment

Find an ANTONYM for each underlined word. Circle the letter of your answer.

14. alienate

    a befriend

    b familiarize

    c clarify

    d reveal

15. forbearance

    a cowardice

    b impatience

    c envy

    d vanity

16. overt

    a hearty

    b narrow

    c ancient

    d secret

17. recant

    a confirm

    b whisper

    c straighten

    d praise

18. <u>reproach</u>

    a   departure

    b   honor

    c   freshness

    d   immaturity

Find the words that correctly complete each analogy. Circle the letter of your answer.

19. clean : immaculate ::

    a   chore : <u>servile</u>

    b   servant : <u>servile</u>

    c   honest : <u>servile</u>

    d   humble : <u>servile</u>

20. peep : screech ::

    a   stage : <u>ovation</u>

    b   applause : <u>ovation</u>

    c   audience : <u>ovation</u>

    d   performers : <u>ovation</u>

21. inaugurate : governor ::

    a   <u>ordain</u> : president

    b   <u>ordain</u> : rabbi

    c   <u>ordain</u> : teacher

    d   <u>ordain</u> : synagogue

22. happy : joyful ::

    a   embarrassed : <u>fervent</u>

    b   sad : <u>fervent</u>

    c   shy : <u>fervent</u>

    d   eager : <u>fervent</u>

Name: _____   Date: _____

Book 5, Final Test 1 (Lessons 1–20)

Read the passage. Choose the BEST answer for each sentence or question about an under-lined word. Circle the letter of your answer.

CHARLIE CHAPLIN, PART 1

No one has left a more <u>indelible</u> mark on film than Charlie Chaplin. Throughout his <u>prolific</u> 50-year career, Chaplin was a beloved international star. His <u>impeccable</u> comedic timing and cinematic skills came along just as movies were becoming an important art form. With his <u>irrepressible</u> "Little Tramp" character, always clad in a derby hat and loose-fitting pants, Charlie Chaplin showed the world that humor was the true international language.

Charles Spencer Chaplin was born on April 16, 1889, in London, England. His parents separated when he was only a year old, and he was raised by his mother. Though his mother suffered from mental illness, she inspired her young son. Before her illness, she was a music hall performer, and, apparently, she <u>bequeathed</u> to Charlie her talents for humor, singing, and dancing. As a child, Charlie developed an <u>ardent</u> love for performing. Though he worked various jobs onstage and off to help support his family, he soon decided to become an entertainer himself.

At first Charlie worked for a <u>pittance</u> as a performer in assorted dance troops and musical theater companies. One of these, the Fred Karno Company, had a huge impact on his comedic development. In 1910 and 1912, Charlie toured the U.S. with the Karno group. During the tour, producer Mack Sennett, the patri-arch of American silent film comedy, happened to catch the show. Sennett was impressed with Charlie's <u>agile</u> manner on stage and knew that he had found a great talent. Sennett hired Chaplin right away. A new <u>epoch</u> in screen comedy was about to begin.

Chaplin made his film debut in 1914 with *Making A Living*. He then starred in a string of films, most of them <u>vignettes</u>. Soon Chaplin wanted more control of his movies. He began directing with his thirteenth film, *Caught in the Rain*. Even in 1915 when he began working with a new film company, Essanay, Chap-lin kept creative control over his work. Chaplin, the <u>indefatigable</u> genius, turned out hit after hit. Among his most <u>renowned</u> early comedies are *The Rink, Easy Street, The Cure, The Immigrant, Sunnyside, The Idle Class*, and the full-length masterpiece *The Kid*. During these years, Charlie developed his Little Tramp character into the compassionate figure loved by audiences around the world. People around the world could identify with the Little Tramp and were inspired by his eternal optimism. Chaplin perfected his unique style. He combined acrobatic grace, expressive gestures, and flawless comic timing.

1. Read this sentence from the passage.

No one has left a more <u>indelible</u> mark on film than Charlie Chaplin.

In this sentence, <u>indelible</u> means

   a   permanent.
   b   honorable.
   c   charming.
   d   gifted.

2. Read this sentence from the passage.

Throughout his <u>prolific</u> 50-year career, Chaplin was a beloved international star.

<u>Prolific</u> means abundantly

   a   talented.
   b   productive.
   c   successful.
   d   humorous.

3. Read this sentence from the passage.

His <u>impeccable</u> comedic timing and cinematic skills came along just as movies were becoming an important art form.

In this sentence, <u>impeccable</u> means

   a   amazing.
   b   hilarious.
   c   flawless.
   d   extraordinary.

4. Read this sentence from the passage.

With his <u>irrepressible</u> "Little Tramp" character, always clad in a derby hat and loose-fitting pants, Charlie Chaplin showed the world that humor was the true international language.

In this sentence, <u>irrepressible</u> means

   a   unforgettable.
   b   incapable of being held back.
   c   internationally known.
   d   shy and curious.

5. Read these words from the passage.

   . . . and apparently she <u>bequeathed</u> to Charlie her talents for humor, singing, and dancing.

   This sentence means that Charlie's mother

   a   encouraged Charlie to develop his talents.

   b   passed her talents down to Charlie.

   c   demonstrated her humor, singing, and dancing to Charlie.

   d   took Charlie to see comedians, singers, and dancers.

6. Read this sentence from the passage.

   As a child, Charlie developed an <u>ardent</u> love for performing.

   An <u>ardent</u> love is

   a   shy.

   b   gentle.

   c   secret.

   d   passionate.

7. Read this sentence from the passage.

   At first Charlie worked for a <u>pittance</u> as a performer in assorted dance troops and musical theater companies.

   In this sentence, <u>pittance</u> means

   a   a very small amount of money.

   b   room and board.

   c   an adequate amount of money.

   d   theatrical manager.

8. Read this sentence from the passage.

   Sennett was impressed with Charlie's <u>agile</u> manner on stage and knew that he had found a great talent.

   In this sentence, <u>agile</u> means

   a   ability to move quickly and easily.

   b   funny.

   c   calm and composed.

   d   serious.

9. Read this sentence from the passage.

A new epoch in screen comedy was about to begin.

In this sentence, an epoch means

a an actor.

b a movie.

c an era.

d a style.

10. Read this sentence from the passage.

He then starred in a string of films, most of them vignettes.

In this sentence, vignettes means

a short movies that provide a clear picture.

b short poems that provide a clear picture.

c small paintings with remarkable details.

d small sculptures with remarkable details.

11. Read this sentence from the passage.

Chaplin, the indefatigable genius, turned out hit after hit.

In this sentence, indefatigable means

a amazing.

b amiable.

c brilliant.

d tireless.

12. Read these words from the passage.

Among his most renowned early comedies are *The Rink, Easy Street . . .*

In this sentence, renowned means

a extraordinary.

b enjoyable.

c famous.

d skillful.

Book 5, Final Test 2 (Lessons 1–20)

Read the passage. Choose the BEST answer for each sentence or question about an under-lined word. Circle the letter of your answer.

CHARLIE CHAPLIN, PART 2

By the 1920s, Charlie was one of the most famous and <u>affluent</u> movie stars in the world. Although he had no trouble finding well-paying work with various studios, Chaplin wanted to have complete freedom to control his work. Along with a few other big stars, he formed United Artists, the first film studio owned and operated by actors. Several <u>sublime</u> classics followed, including *The Gold Rush, The Circus, City Lights,* and *Modern Times.* Although talking pictures were introduced in 1928, Chaplin feared that speech would detract from his Little Tramp character and resisted making talking pictures until 1940. In that year, he made *The Great Dictator,* which ridiculed Adolf Hitler at the beginning of World War II. He won three Oscars for *The Great Dictator,* but waited seven years before releasing his next picture, *Monsieur Verdoux.* His next picture was *Limelight,* a look back to the music hall world of his youth.

Limelight, made in 1952, was the last film Charlie made in America. During the 1950s, some politicians tried to <u>discredit</u> Chaplin. Their <u>strident</u> voices accused him of disloyalty to the United States. The FBI collected over 1,900 pages of information on Chaplin. All of Charlie's <u>prestige</u> couldn't protect him from these unfair attacks, and he became lonely and depressed. In the end, Charlie <u>renounced</u> America, settling permanently in Switzerland with his wife, Oona, and their children.

Before he retired, Chaplin's film career <u>culminated</u> with *A King in New York* (1957) and *A Countess from Hong Kong* (1967). He spent his final years writing his <u>memoirs</u>, composing music for his films and enjoying a happy family life. In 1972 he briefly returned to the United States to receive several tributes, including a special Academy Award. On Oscar night that year, he earned a thunderous <u>ovation</u> for his remarkable contributions to the film industry. Charlie Chaplin died on Christmas Day in 1977 at the age of eighty-eight.

Today, Chaplin's <u>legacy</u> is admired the world over. <u>Connoisseurs</u> of film readily acknowledge Chaplin as one of the greatest screen artists of all time. His <u>innovations</u> in film comedy, blending broad physical antics with tender emotion,

have never been equaled. Thanks to videotapes and DVDs, audiences today
continue to laugh at the Little Tramp. Nearly one hundred years after he first
appeared, this charming character remains one of the world's most enduring
screen personalities.

1. Charlie Chaplin became famous and <u>affluent</u>. An <u>affluent</u> person is very

   a rich.

   b talented.

   c well-loved.

   d well-educated.

2. The passage states that many of Chaplin's movies are <u>sublime</u>. <u>Sublime</u> means

   a innovative.

   b worth examining.

   c absolutely splendid.

   d difficult to understand.

3. During the 1950s, some politicians tried to <u>discredit</u> Charlie Chaplin. This means that
   they tried to

   a make him pay higher taxes.

   b hire him to make speeches for them.

   c steal his acting secrets.

   d ruin his reputation.

4. <u>Strident</u> voices are

   a harsh.

   b heroic.

   c low and gentle.

   d deep and melodious.

5. Charlie's <u>prestige</u> could not protect him from unfair accusations. His <u>prestige</u>

   a was his film career.

   b was the respect he had earned for his accomplishments.

   c were his family, friends, and colleagues in the movie business.

   d were the politicians who were on his side.

6. Chaplin <u>renounced</u> America and went to live in Switzerland. This means that he

    a   rejected or gave up America.

    b   chose never to come back to America.

    c   forgot America.

    d   happily left America.

7. In the passage, <u>culminated</u> means

    a   destroyed itself.

    b   slipped away.

    c   began triumphantly.

    d   reached its climax.

8. When Charlie Chaplin wrote his <u>memoirs,</u> he wrote

    a   a how-to article about the movie business.

    b   a fictional story about actors and actresses.

    c   about his own personal experiences.

    d   a group of poems about silent films.

9. An <u>ovation</u> is

    a   a few people clapping.

    b   long and loud applause.

    c   something new.

    d   something original.

10. In the passage, "Chaplin's <u>legacy</u>" means

    a   the money that Chaplin left to his family in his will.

    b   the gifts, such as his films, that Chaplin passed down to those who came after him.

    c   the property that Chaplin owned at the time of his death.

    d   the memoirs that Chaplin wrote about his life.

11. <u>Connoisseurs</u> of film are

    a   famous movie stars.

    b   wealthy movie producers.

    c   people with extensive knowledge of film.

    d   people who have seen most of the latest movies.

12. <u>Innovations</u> in film comedy

    a   always receive loud and long applause.

    b   are actors who appear in movie comedies.

    c   are new or original ideas or changes in film comedy.

    d   are rules that most film directors follow when making comedies.

Book 5, Final Test 3 (Lessons 1–20)

Read the passage. Choose the BEST answer for each sentence or question about an underlined word. Circle the letter of your answer.

THE GREAT SAN FRANCISCO EARTHQUAKE AND FIRE, PART 1

By the early 1900s, San Francisco had become one of America's most <u>picturesque</u> cities. <u>Ornate</u> Victorian homes, steep hills, and a bustling downtown enhanced San Francisco's reputation as the jewel of the West Coast. However, all that changed one spring day in 1906. A powerful earthquake, followed by several huge fires, nearly <u>razed</u> the city. This was one of the worst natural disasters in American history.

Fire had <u>engulfed</u> the city on six previous occasions. Each time, San Franciscans had rebuilt their city. Leaders from the fire department and other local agencies understood how <u>susceptible</u> the city was to fire danger. At the time, most of San Francisco's structures were made of wood and other highly <u>combustible</u> materials. Many homeowners, landlords, and business owners were guilty of <u>flagrant</u> fire code violations. As precautionary measures, they installed extra hydrants and underground water tanks called cisterns. But no one had ever <u>contemplated</u> the kind of calamity that began at 5:12 on the morning of April 18, 1906.

At that time, a strong earthquake jolted the city awake. The quake was felt as far north as Oregon and as far south as Los Angeles, and the tremors lasted between forty and sixty seconds. A major quake is bad enough, but many other misfortunes <u>conspired</u> to worsen the situation. In one cruel twist of fate, fire chief Dennis Sullivan was fatally injured in the earthquake, depriving the city of his leadership. Many of the firemen in the downtown district had just returned from a three-alarm fire in the city when the earthquake hit. Already exhausted, they had to immediately return to work when the earthquake <u>simultaneously</u> ignited 52 separate fires in different parts of the city. Tragically, the quake also destroyed San Francisco's fire alarm system. Not a single fire alarm sounded during the entire ordeal.

San Francisco's water reservoirs were located twenty miles from the city. Six miles of that distance was on the earthquake's fault line. This was a major hindrance to firefighters. To make things worse, the quake completely destroyed many of the city's underground water pipes. Backup pipelines turned out to be ineffectual as well. Firefighters tried to access hydrant after hydrant without getting a drop of water. Firefighters had to draw water from emergency cisterns, which soon went dry. In desperation, firefighters tried to get water from city sewers.

1. Read this sentence from the passage.

   By the early 1900s, San Francisco had become one of America's most picturesque cities.
   In this sentence, picturesque means

   a artistic.
   b beautiful.
   c prosperous.
   d famous.

2. Read these words from the passage.
   Ornate Victorian homes . . .
   In this sentence, ornate means

   a expensive.
   b colorful.
   c elaborately decorated.
   d lovely and old-fashioned.

3. Read this sentence from the passage.

   A powerful earthquake, followed by several huge fires, nearly razed the city.
   In this sentence, razed means

   a destroyed.
   b terrified.
   c bankrupted.
   d attacked.

4. Read this sentence from the passage.

   Fire had engulfed the city on six previous occasions.
   In this sentence, engulfed means

   a overwhelmed.
   b frightened.
   c challenged.
   d approached.

5. Read this sentence from the passage.

   Leaders from the fire department and other local agencies understood how <u>susceptible</u> the city was to fire danger.

   In this sentence, <u>susceptible</u> means

   a close.
   b vulnerable.
   c terrified.
   d wary.

6. Read this sentence from the passage.

   But no one had ever <u>contemplated</u> the kind of calamity that began at 5:12 on the morning of April 18, 1906.

   In this sentence, <u>contemplated</u> means

   a feared.
   b escaped.
   c fought.
   d thought about.

7. Read this sentence from the passage.

   A major quake is bad enough, but many other misfortunes <u>conspired</u> to worsen the situation.

   In this sentence, <u>conspired</u> means

   a planned.
   b came together.
   c threatened.
   d happened.

8. Read this sentence from the passage.

   At the time, most of San Francisco's structures were made of wood and other highly <u>combustible</u> materials.

   In this sentence, <u>combustible</u> means

   a weak.
   b oily.
   c flammable.
   d suspicious.

9. Read this sentence from the passage.

Many homeowners, landlords, and business owners were guilty of <u>flagrant</u> fire code violations.

In this sentence, <u>flagrant</u> means

a sneaky.

b careless.

c intentional.

d clearly bad.

10. Read these words from the passage.

. . . when the earthquake <u>simultaneously</u> ignited 52 separate fires in different parts of the city.

In this sentence, <u>simultaneously</u> means

a accidentally.

b tragically.

c at the same time.

d in the same place.

11. Read this sentence from the passage.

This was a major <u>hindrance</u> to firefighters.

A <u>hindrance</u> is anything that

a is an obstacle.

b upsets people.

c kills people.

d makes people realize how tragic a situation is.

12. Read this sentence from the passage.

Backup pipelines turned out to be <u>ineffectual</u> as well.

In this sentence, <u>ineffectual</u> means

a broken.

b not having the desired result.

c burned.

d not available in time.

Book 5, Final Test 4 (Lessons 1–20)

Read the passage. Choose the BEST answer for each sentence or question about an underlined word. Circle the letter of your answer.

THE GREAT SAN FRANCISCO EARTHQUAKE AND FIRE, PART 2

Poor communication further <u>stymied</u> the San Francisco Fire Department. Without the ability to communicate, officers could not easily <u>delegate</u> jobs. Many firemen were on their own. Nothing like the disaster they now faced had ever tested these brave men's training and <u>stamina</u>. Exhausted, <u>sweltering</u> in the flames, they did the best they could. Men would occasionally sleep for a few minutes on the ground before getting back up to continue to battle the blaze. It was so hot that it seemed as though the air itself was on fire.

Spreading blazes <u>encroached</u> on every neighborhood. Some thought it would be <u>feasible</u> to put out fires by blowing up burning buildings. The explosions only spread the flames. Many smaller fires came together, forming one grotesque three-mile-long blaze. The fire grew so huge that firefighters drained a 100,000-gallon water cistern without having the slightest impact. The flames raged on relentlessly for three days, causing unimaginable <u>havoc</u>. Slowly, though, firefighters began to win their fight against the blaze. They were helped when the wind changed direction from east to west, blowing the fire back in the direction it had already come. Then came some heavy rains that helped to extinguish the blaze. By April 21, the firefighters had finally triumphed. It did not seem like much of a victory, however. Twenty-three hundred people had perished in the catastrophe. The fire department lost twenty stations and a large <u>cache</u> of equipment. Its highest-ranking officer was dead. But the fire was out at last.

Firefighters' heroic efforts saved much of San Francisco. Soldiers, policemen, and ordinary citizens assisted in the struggle. After the fire, city leaders vowed never to put San Francisco in such a <u>precarious</u> position again. Firefighting innovations helped to protect against a repeat of the 1906 disaster. Today in San Francisco, there are 23 vintage firehouses that <u>commemorate</u> the heroes of 1906. It is not mere <u>rhetoric</u> to say that San Francisco owes its life to them.

Thanks to these intrepid men, and thanks to men and women who followed in their footsteps, the <u>panorama</u> of San Francisco's skyline remains one of the world's most beautiful and well-known cityscapes.

1. Poor communication further <u>stymied</u> the San Francisco Fire Department. This means that poor communication

   a angered firefighters.

   b made it difficult for firefighters to work.

   c caused firefighters to lose their lives.

   d alienated firefighters from one another.

2. To <u>delegate</u> jobs is to

   a assign them.

   b do them well.

   c do them sloppily.

   d be unable to do them.

3. <u>Stamina</u> is the ability to

   a think quickly.

   b give tasks to others.

   c withstand hardship.

   d care about other people's welfare.

4. Firefighters <u>sweltered</u> as they worked. This means that they

   a felt exhausted.

   b perspired

   c suffered from great heat.

   d worked as hard as they could.

5. To <u>encroach</u> on a neighborhood is to

   a work there.

   b engulf it instantly.

   c encircle it.

   d go over its boundaries.

6. Something that is <u>feasible</u> is

   a   challenging.

   b   doable.

   c   wildly successful.

   d   doubtful.

7. In the passage, <u>havoc</u> means

   a   devastation.

   b   fury.

   c   fear.

   d   heat.

8. In the passage, "a <u>cache</u> of equipment" means

   a   stolen equipment.

   b   needed equipment.

   c   equipment that someone has stored.

   d   equipment that someone has just purchased.

9. In the passage, "a <u>precarious</u> position" means

   a   an embarrassing position.

   b   an illegal position.

   c   a position that is too high above the ground.

   d   an unsafe position.

10. To <u>commemorate</u> heroes is to

   a   remember and honor them.

   b   cheer for them.

   c   vote for them in elections.

   d   ask for their autographs.

11. In the passage, <u>rhetoric</u> means

   a   gratefulness.

   b   exaggerated or insincere language.

   c   exaggerated emotion.

   d   the art of using language skillfully.

12. The <u>panorama</u> of San Francisco's skyline is

    a   a postcard of its skyline.

    b   an obstructed view of its skyline.

    c   a skyline of ruined buildings.

    d   a full view of its skyline.

Answer Key

Lesson 1 Test

1. C
2. C
3. B
4. A
5. C
6. A
7. B
8. C
9. B
10. D
11. B
12. D
13. A
14. C
15. C
16. A
17. D
18. A
19. A
20. C
21. D
22. D
23. A
24. B
25. B
26. A
27. A
28. C
29. C
30. B
31. B
32. C

Lesson 2 Test

1. C
2. D
3. A
4. C
5. D
6. A
7. D
8. B
9. B
10. A
11. D
12. C
13. D
14. A
15. B
16. A
17. D
18. B
19. C
20. A
21. B
22. B
23. D
24. C
25. D
26. A
27. D
28. B
29. B
30. C
31. A
32. A

Lesson 3 Test

1. C
2. A
3. A
4. D
5. B
6. C
7. B
8. A
9. A
10. D
11. C
12. D
13. C
14. A
15. D
16. B
17. C
18. B
19. A
20. C
21. D
22. A
23. C
24. D
25. B
26. A
27. B
28. B
29. C
30. C

Lesson 4 Test

1. D
2. B
3. A
4. A
5. B
6. C
7. D
8. A
9. C
10. D
11. B
12. B
13. C
14. B
15. D
16. A
17. C
18. A
19. B
20. D
21. B
22. D
23. A
24. B
25. A
26. D
27. D

Lesson 5 Test

1. A
2. C
3. A
4. D
5. A
6. D
7. B
8. D
9. C
10. A
11. B
12. D
13. B
14. D
15. C
16. C
17. A
18. D
19. B
20. B

Lesson 6 Test

21. D
22. A
23. B
24. A

1. A
2. C
3. B
4. B
5. A
6. B
7. D
8. C
9. A
10. C
11. B
12. A
13. B
14. A
15. C
16. B
17. C
18. D
19. C
20. A
21. C
22. D
23. A
24. C
25. A

Lesson 7 Test

1. D
2. B
3. B
4. A
5. C
6. B
7. B
8. A
9. B
10. C
11. A
12. A
13. C
14. D
15. A
16. D
17. B
18. A

Answer Key

19. B
20. C
21. D
22. C
23. D
24. B
25. D
26. B

Lesson 8 Test

1. A
2. C
3. A
4. B
5. A
6. B
7. D
8. B
9. D
10. A
11. C
12. D
13. D
14. C
15. C
16. A
17. C
18. B
19. B
20. D
21. A

Lesson 9 Test

1. D
2. B
3. C
4. B
5. B
6. A
7. A
8. C
9. D
10. A
11. C
12. D
13. C
14. A
15. D
16. B
17. D
18. C

19. B
20. A
21. D
22. C
23. C
24. B
25. D

Lesson 10 Test

1. A
2. B
3. C
4. B
5. D
6. A
7. D
8. C
9. B
10. C
11. D
12. C
13. B
14. A
15. C
16. B
17. C
18. D
19. A
20. D
21. B
22. B

**Midterm Test 1
(Lessons 1–10)**

1. B
2. B
3. C
4. A
5. B
6. D
7. C
8. C
9. A
10. A
11. B
12. C

**Midterm Test 2
(Lessons 1–10)**

1. B

2. A
3. C
4. C
5. D
6. A
7. B
8. C
9. A
10. B
11. D
12. A

Lesson 11 Test

1. C
2. C
3. B
4. C
5. B
6. D
7. B
8. A
9. D
10. C
11. A
12. B
13. C
14. D
15. C
16. D
17. C
18. A
19. B
20. D
21. B
22. A
23. D
24. B
25. A
26. C

Lesson 12 Test

1. B
2. A
3. B
4. B
5. A
6. C
7. C
8. D
9. A
10. B

11. D
12. A
13. A
14. C
15. D
16. C
17. B
18. A
19. B
20. D
21. B
22. B

Lesson 13 Test

1. A
2. D
3. B
4. C
5. B
6. D
7. D
8. A
9. D
10. A
11. B
12. C
13. D
14. D
15. A
16. B
17. C
18. C
19. D
20. B
21. A
22. D
23. C

Lesson 14 Test

1. A
2. B
3. B
4. C
5. D
6. C
7. D
8. C
9. A
10. D
11. A
12. B

Answer Key

13. D
14. B
15. A
16. C
17. A
18. B
19. D
20. B
21. C
22. B
23. D

Lesson 15 Test

1. D
2. C
3. D
4. B
5. B
6. D
7. C
8. A
9. D
10. B
11. C
12. D
13. A
14. B
15. D
16. B
17. C
18. D
19. B
20. A

Lesson 16 Test

1. B
2. A
3. B
4. A
5. B
6. D
7. C
8. A
9. B
10. D
11. C
12. C
13. D
14. A
15. B
16. A

17. C
18. D
19. C
20. C
21. B

Lesson 17 Test

1. C
2. D
3. C
4. B
5. B
6. C
7. D
8. A
9. C
10. B
11. D
12. A
13. B
14. B
15. A
16. C
17. A
18. C
19. B
20. D
21. C
22. C

Lesson 18 Test

1. D
2. A
3. A
4. B
5. D
6. A
7. A
8. C
9. D
10. C
11. C
12. B
13. A
14. C
15. B
16. C
17. D
18. B
19. B
20. C

21. A

Lesson 19 Test

1. B
2. B
3. B
4. D
5. C
6. B
7. D
8. D
9. C
10. A
11. D
12. A
13. C
14. D
15. B
16. D
17. A
18. A
19. C
20. D
21. B
22. D
23. C

Lesson 20 Test

1. B
2. C
3. D
4. C
5. C
6. B
7. B
8. C
9. D
10. B
11. C
12. A
13. A
14. A
15. B
16. D
17. A
18. B
19. D
20. B
21. B
22. D

Final Test 1
(Lessons 1–20)

1. A
2. B
3. C
4. B
5. B
6. D
7. A
8. A
9. C
10. A
11. D
12. C

Final Test 2
(Lessons 1–20)

1. A
2. C
3. D
4. A
5. B
6. A
7. D
8. C
9. B
10. B
11. C
12. C

Final Test 3
(Lessons 1–20)

1. B
2. C
3. A
4. A
5. B
6. D
7. B
8. C
9. D
10. C
11. A
12. B

Answer Key

Final Test 4
(Lessons 1–20)

1. B
2. A
3. C
4. C
5. C
6. B
7. A
8. C
9. D
10. A
11. B
12. D